Ludwig Beethoven
and the Chiming Tower Bells
Study Guide

By Judy Wilcox

Zeezok
publishing

Elyria, OH

Ludwig Beethoven
and the Chiming Tower Bells
Study Guide

ISBN 0-9746505-7-9
© 2005 by Zeezok Publishing

Published by:
Zeezok Publishing
PO Box 1960
Elyria, OH 44036

www.Zeezok.com
1-800-749-1681

Map of the major cities Beethoven visited

Beethoven's World and Place in Musical History

Middle Ages	450 – 1450
Renaissance	1450 – 1600
Baroque	1600 – 1750
Classical *(Beethoven born 1770)*	**1750 – 1820**
Romantic *(Beethoven died 1827)*	**1820 – 1900**
20th Century or New Music	1900 – Present

1770

On December 16, Ludwig van Beethoven is born in Bonn, Germany. The "Boston Massacre" occurs between civilians and British troops in the American colonies. In Paris, the first public restaurant opens.

On December 24, Beethoven's grandfather (also named Ludwig van Beethoven) dies. The Boston Tea Party, protesting the tea duty, occurs. The waltz becomes fashionable in Vienna.

1773

1774

Beethoven's brother Karl is born. The Continental Congress decides on nonimportation of British goods to American colonies. King Louis XV dies and is succeeded by his grandson, Louis XVI.

Beethoven's second surviving brother, Johann, is born. The Declaration of Independence is passed in the Continental Congress. Captain Cook begins his third voyage to the Pacific.

1776

1777

Fire ravages the palace of the Elector at Bonn. American engineer David Bushnell invents the torpedo. The Stars and Stripes are adopted as the Continental Congress flag.

On March 26, Beethoven gives a public concert in Cologne, Germany. American colonies sign treaties with France and Holland, and reject the British peace offer. James Cook discovers Hawaii.

1778

1779

Beethoven receives musical lessons from Pfeiffer (piano), Ries (violin), and Brother Willibald Koch and Zenser (organ). The British surrender to colonial troops at Vincennes, Indiana, ending British control of the west during the Revolutionary War. Stephen Decatur, U.S. naval hero, is born.

Beethoven is taken out of school, at age 11, by his father.

1781

4

Chapter One

Reading Comprehension Questions

1. What neighbor and family member lived across the street from Ludwig's house in Bonn?
   • His grandfather, Grandfather Beethoven, his dear companion, pp. 11, 14.

2. What was Ludwig's father's job?
   • Father Johann sang in the Elector's royal choir at the palace, and he gave violin and piano lessons, p. 11.

3. Can you recall the two instruments Ludwig learned to play at an early age?
   • Piano and violin, p. 16.

4. Name or list some ways that Ludwig "escaped" from the exhausting hours of music practice his father required of him.
   • He played in the garden with neighbor children, p. 17; he sat on the window seat in his house and dreamed, p. 19; he listened to the carillon, or bells, at the palace tower, pp. 19–20; he flew kites, p. 23.

5. Why would neighbors of the Beethovens often meet at their home in the evening?
   • Impromptu concerts, pp. 11, 21.

6. One night the carillon began ringing in the late night hours. What happened?
   • The bell tower caught fire and the carillon crashed to the ground, p. 22.

7. Why did Father Johann remove Ludwig from school at age eleven?
   • He wanted Ludwig to focus on his music, p. 31.

8. When did Ludwig sometimes have his music lessons — particularly under Herr Pfeiffer and his father?
   • In the middle of the night, after being awakened from his sleep, p. 27.

Character Qualities

Hard-working (pp. 16, 24, 27) – Ludwig spent many wearying hours practicing the piano and the violin so he could be "another Mozart some day," p. 16. He devoted hours daily to practicing scales and difficult exercises, p. 18. He also wanted to help his family financially so that his mother wouldn't have to work so hard; this meant even longer hours of practice. Sometimes the hard work was forced on him during the late night hours under his father and Herr Pfeiffer's demanding eyes, p. 27.

Helpful (pp. 18, 24, 31) – Whether he was drawing water for his mother, practicing diligently for a concert at the palace, or leaving school to go on a concert tour, Ludwig devoted himself to helping his family.

Attentive (pp. 14, 19, 21, 28) – Ludwig was particularly attentive to his loved ones and to music. Ludwig relished time with his grandfather, listening to the older Kapellmeister's stories. He was always attuned to hearing the carillon ringing, and he enjoyed the music of the impromptu concerts at the Beethoven home. He was attentive to the details needed to *write* music, as well.

Imaginative (pp. 19, 29) – Ludwig enjoyed sitting alone at the window seat where he could dream of faraway lands and let wonderful melodies creep into his mind. Later, Ludwig was imaginative in that he played music that didn't follow the rules of music. He dreamed of and dared to play music "just as it sang itself in his mind," p. 29.

Tidbits of Interest

Page 9 – Bonn is a city on the Rhine River (also spelled Rhein), south of Cologne in Germany. In the 13th century, Bonn became the capital of the Electorate of Cologne. At Beethoven's birth, Germany was made of small states ruled by Electors who lived like royalty. During the Middle Ages, groups of princes were chosen to elect the emperor of the country. These Electors, or princes, had considerable power and presided over their own courts. In 1815, still in Ludwig's lifetime, Bonn was awarded to Prussia, and later, in 1949 (after World War II), it was chosen as the capital for West Germany. Bonn is in the Rhine valley below the Seven Mountains or Seven Hills, a range of seven peaks in the area. Ruined castles sit on three hilltops along the Rhine near Bonn.[1]

Pages 10, 20 – Gasse means alley, lane, or cobbled street in German. Bonngasse and Rhinegasse are only a few streets apart, but Rhinegasse was closer to the river. On Bonngasse, the Beethovens lived in rooms above the Fischer family's house.[2]

Pages 10, 12 – Grandfather Louis (or Ludwig) Beethoven had moved from Antwerp, Holland, first working as a bass singer for the Elector of Cologne, and then rising to Kapellmeister, or senior musician, for the Court. Young Ludwig was only three years old when his grandfather died (December 24, 1773).

Page 11 – Ludwig was baptized in St. Remigius Church, the same Roman Catholic church in which his parents were married. Though Beethoven did not attend church regularly,[3] he is recognized as an intensely religious man.[4]

Page 14 – Herr Ries was a Bonn neighbor named Franz Ries who taught Beethoven the violin, and whose son, Ferdinand Ries, became a close friend to Ludwig. Herr Simrock, the horn player, was Nikolaus Simrock who later became Beethoven's Bonn music publisher.

Page 15 – Gottfried Fischer, the son of the Beethovens' landlord, wrote a diary of remembrances about the Beethoven family. Fischer's mother, Cacilia, told Gottfried that Beethoven played from a small bench when his father first started giving him lessons.[5]

Page 16 – Johann, Ludwig's father, was appointed to the post of Court Tenor and gave violin and piano lessons. Though Johann wanted Ludwig to play concerts like Mozart and bring their family wealth, Ludwig was not the natural prodigy that Mozart or Handel had been. Nevertheless, Beethoven's father made him study music for hours every day. When given the opportunity, Ludwig would play with neighborhood children in the Fischers' courtyard, in the palace garden, and in the sand along the Rhine River.[6]

Page 19 – Frau is the German equivalent to *Mrs*. Ludwig's mother was named Anna Maria Magdelena Keferig (or Keverich) and was described as tall, with earnest eyes and polite manners. She was well respected and a good domestic woman who would sew, knit, and pay the rent and baker's bills promptly.[7] The Beethovens had seven children, only three of whom survived infancy.

A carillon is a set of at least twenty-three cast bronze bells that are fixed and tuned chromatically. While the bells are sounded by hammers, they are controlled from a keyboard. They are usually located in a tower. In this biography, the carillon was in the Elector's palace tower.

Page 20 – The old red ferry called the flying bridge was a ferry that moved across the river without man or animal power. A strong rope (nearly 1,000 feet long) was anchored in the middle of the river and then was tied to the mast of a ferry at the height of about twenty feet. This rope was held out of the water by several small hulls (or boat-like floats) that helped keep the rope from wearing out. The ferry would start from one bank of the river by taking a diagonal yaw position. The rudder maintained an angle so that the current would push the ferry sideways. This pendulum motion allowed the ferry to swing from bank to bank. There is still such a ferry, named the *Flying Bridge*, in fact, in operation at the crossing of the Rhine near Bonn.

Page 22 – A fire destroyed a large portion of the Elector's palace in 1777. The Beethovens moved back above the Fischers' shortly after the fire.

Page 23 – Benjamin Franklin's famous kite experiment had occurred in 1752 and ignited, or sparked, an interest in kite-flying around the world.

Page 24 –When Ludwig gave his first concert in Bonn, the false age of six was listed as his age. It was probably an age given by his father so Ludwig would seem to be more of a musical prodigy like Mozart. The Elector at this point was Maximilian Friedrich, who had employed Beethoven's grandfather as Kapellmeister.[8] This description of Ludwig's special costume for his first concert in Bonn was apparently the gala dress of all court musicians that year.[9] Electors often established orchestras for their own pleasure and to entertain guests.

Page 27 – Herr Pfeiffer was Tobias Pfeiffer, a twenty-nine-year-old actor and musician (and tavern buddy of Johann Beethoven's) who would awaken Ludwig in the middle of the night to make him practice the piano.[10] No wonder neighbors recall the boy weeping before the piano.[11]

Page 31 – Beethoven was only eleven when his formal education ended. He had attended primary schools — Neugasse, Münsterschule, and Tirocinium — but his father pulled him from school in 1781 to focus on his musical career.

1782 – 1784

1782

Beethoven's first pieces are published, the "Dressler March Variations" for piano. He becomes deputy court organist to Neefe, and his friendship with Wegeler and the von Breuning family begins. Thomas Greenville is sent from London to Paris to open peace talks with B. Franklin. Spain completes its conquest of Florida. The Montgolfier brothers construct a hot air balloon.

1783

Beethoven travels with his mother to Rotterdam. The Peace of Versailles is signed, and Britain recognizes the independence of the United States. Famine breaks out in Japan. Simon Bolivar, a Latin-American soldier-statesman, is born.

1784

Beethoven becomes Neefe's assistant officially. Elector Maximilian Friedrich dies and is succeeded by Maximilian Franz, Empress Maria Theresa's son. Great Britain signs a peace treaty with Tippoo Sahib of Mysore. Scottish millwright Andrew Meikle invents the threshing machine.

Chapter Two

Reading Comprehension Questions

1. Mother Beethoven and Ludwig sailed down the Rhine River to what country and why?
   • To Holland, to give musical concerts for the royal families, pp. 33–34.

2. When he returned to Bonn, what new musical instrument did Ludwig learn to play? And do you remember his first teacher's name on that instrument?
   • He learned to play the organ, and his teacher's name was Brother Willibald, pp. 35, 37.

3. When he later took organ lessons from Zenser at the Münsterkirche, Ludwig wrote his own compositions. What did Zenser see as a "problem" with those works, and what was Ludwig's response to the difficulty Zenser pointed out?
   • The music was too hard for Ludwig's small hands; however, Ludwig determined that he would simply play it when he was bigger, pp. 39–40.

4. Do you remember the names of Ludwig's younger brothers?
   • Karl and Johann, p. 41.

5. How did Ludwig and his family celebrate his mother's birthday?
   • They made a special bower of birthday flowers for her, gave her a concert with the neighbors, and danced and enjoyed music all night, pp. 41–43.

6. What major musician from the court did Ludwig next study under, practicing Bach's difficult works, in particular? And how did this musician describe Ludwig's future?
   • He studied with organist Herr Neefe, pp. 46–47. Neefe predicted that Ludwig would be another Mozart some day, p. 49.

7. As a youth, what conducting position did Ludwig undertake, and was he successful?
   • He became court conductor for the theater orchestra, p. 62. His own orchestra applauded him for his leadership, p. 63.

8. Can you provide an anecdote (or a story) from this chapter that shows Ludwig was a bit of a tease?
   • He challenged the soloist, Herr Heller, in chapel to stay on his part while Ludwig attempted to throw him off with his accompaniment, p. 65.

Character Qualities

Diligent (pp. 37, 39, 47, 63) – Playing an organ as a young man was not an easy task, but Ludwig never shrank from the job and even learned how to play the bass notes with the foot pedals. Ludwig practiced diligently for the chapel services, memorizing the music, playing for the early morning services, and playing for special services at another nearby church. He learned difficult pieces, composition rules, and writing variations to improve his musical abilities. Furthermore, he proved that even as a young lad, he understood the necessity of patient, diligent practice of difficult passages when he conducted the theater orchestra.

Respect for Others (pp. 41, 44, 47, 65) – His treatment of his mother, particularly honoring her on her birthday, demonstrated his deep respect for his mother. And he was glad for a yearly income so that his mother would not have to work so hard, p. 65. Ludwig's appreciation for the skill of other musicians, such as the court organist Herr Neefe, showed respect for others. He even agreed to Neefe's rules and composition requirements although it saddened him not to be able to write variations as he heard them in his mind. Ludwig also recognized that the Elector deserved respect and bowed low to him, p. 65.

Leadership (pp. 38, 49, 62) – Even as a young man, Ludwig was given important responsibilities: playing for church services and for the court chapel when the senior organist was absent, and taking on the role of conductor for the theater orchestra. He took on that role in spite of the fact that many musicians expected the task to be too difficult for a child. By the end of the first rehearsal, however, they applauded the young conductor and appreciated his leadership.

Visionary (pp. 39–40, 47) – Ludwig composed music that he couldn't even play because his hands were not large enough, but it didn't deter his enthusiasm for composing, and he even expressed an attitude of, "I'll play it when I'm bigger." He had a view of the future even as a youngster. He practiced and experimented with the organ, and he risked writing music that didn't "follow the rules" for composing variations. His visionary quality transformed music forever!

12

Tidbits of Interest

Page 33 – This portion of the chapter is an excellent opportunity for a bit of geography study. The Rhine River is one of the longest rivers in Europe, and it begins in Switzerland flowing north and east approximately 820 miles, but it can also be navigated from the North Sea to Basel, Switzerland. Almost eighty percent of its ship-carrying waters pass through Germany, although not all oceangoing vessels can go the entire distance on the Rhine. Many ships must end their journey in Cologne, Germany (near Bonn). From Cologne, cargo must then go by barges pushed by smaller ships until the Rhine reaches the intersection of the three countries of France, Germany, and Switzerland. During the Middle Ages and beyond, feudal lords and landowners built castles along the Rhine to protect their lands from marauders and land-grabbing neighbors. There are more castles on the short stretch of river from the city of Mainz to Bonn, a length of only thirty-five miles, than there are in any other river valley in the world.

Page 34 – Rotterdam is a port city in the Netherlands province of South Holland. Currently, Rotterdam has the second largest port in the world (after Shanghai). Much of the Netherlands is flat, about half of its surface area being less than four feet above sea level, and large areas are below sea level. An extensive system of dykes and canals is used to protect these low areas from flooding. Windmills are used to pump water out of low areas in which a water level must be maintained, which explains why Holland (a province in the Netherlands) is commonly associated with windmills.

Page 35 – Beethoven studied organ with Brother Willibald Koch from the Franciscan monastery in Bonn. Brother Willibald eventually accepted Beethoven as his assistant. Playing organs in Ludwig's time required lots of physical activity and strength. The organ is a keyboard instrument in which sound is produced by air passing through pipes of various size and construction to give a wide variety of pitches and timbres. In Beethoven's time, bellows attached to foot pedals were the means of forcing air through the pipes of the organ. But even as a child, Ludwig was known as a boy of musical ambition and physical strength.[12]

Page 39 – Ludwig played special music for a Minorite church in the area. The Minorite Order is a Roman Catholic order founded by St. Francis of Assisi, and the order is dedicated to charities, preaching, and missions. Münsterkirche, also known as Münster Cathedral, is located in central Bonn. It is made of gray stone and is a landmark in the city with its five distinctive towers, or spires. Herr Zenser was the church organist for Münsterkirche.

Page 40 – Ludwig loved experimenting with the organ and writing new compositions. In fact, even as a youth he began keeping notebooks of various musical ideas that were crowded in with other ideas in all stages of development — similar to Leonardo da Vinci's notebooks of science and art ideas.[13] These notebooks were masses of corrections and enthusiastic writings, sometimes difficult for anyone but the composer to decipher.[14]

Page 41 – Ludwig's two surviving siblings were his younger brothers Caspar Anton Karl Beethoven (1774–1815) and Nikolaus Johann Beethoven (1776–1848). Karl eventually became a Viennese bank clerk, and Johann became an apothecary and small landowner.

Pages 41–44 – Anyone who knew Ludwig remembered him as always referring to his mother with "love and feeling, calling her often an honest good-hearted woman."[15]

Pages 44–48 – In 1784, the new Elector in Bonn was Maximilian Franz, the youngest brother of Emperor Joseph II. Maximilian Franz was known as the Empress Maria Theresa's youngest and favorite son, and he loved music. He had several chamber groups and orchestras of his own.[16] The Elector's court organist and theater director was Christian Gottlob Neefe (1748–1798), who is described as a Protestant believer who mentored Ludwig.[17] Neefe was a master organist who taught Ludwig classical rules of composition and helped him develop his technique as a keyboard player. Neefe taught Ludwig the *Well-Tempered Clavier* by Bach, which Ludwig still practiced during his years in Vienna. Ludwig always had a deep respect for the music of earlier masters — particularly the music of Bach, Mozart, and Handel.

Page 48 – Ludwig's first published composition, "Nine Variations on a March," came out when he was only twelve years old. Variations are changes to a given theme of music through changes in the melody, harmony, rhythm, or addition to the theme. Ludwig tried to continue publishing music to earn money for his family.[18] Beethoven excelled under Neefe's teaching, and he essentially was apprenticed, or deputized, for the position of Kapellmeister at age twelve![19]

Page 49 – Neefe once wrote in a letter that he thought Ludwig was a genius worthy of and "deserving of help to enable him to travel. He would surely become a second Wolfgang Amadeus Mozart were he to continue as he was begun."[20]

1785 – 1801

Beethoven makes his first visit to Vienna and meets with Mozart. Beethoven's mother dies of consumption, and Beethoven returns to Bonn to provide for his family.

1787

1788
Count Waldstein, life-long friend of Beethoven, arrives in Bonn. Beethoven returns to his old posts of organist and violist in court orchestra.

Beethoven's father retires from the court choir.

1789

1790
Beethoven composes a cantata to honor Emperor Joseph II. Joseph Haydn visits Bonn and shares dinner with court musicians, including Beethoven.

French forces invade Cologne and Bonn, and the court orchestra is abandoned. Beethoven leaves Bonn forever, traveling to Vienna to study under Haydn. Beethoven's father dies in Bonn in December.

1792

1793
Lessons begin with Haydn, and Beethoven first contemplates Schiller's "Ode to Joy" for a musical composition. (It eventually became his theme for his Ninth Symphony in 1824.)

Haydn leaves for London, so Beethoven studies under Albrechtsberger and Salieri.

1794

1795
Beethoven gives his first public performance in Vienna (March 29).

Beethoven takes a concert tour to Prague, Dresden, and Berlin with Prince Lichnowsky.

1796

1797
Signs of Beethoven's deafness are apparent.

Beethoven's First Symphony is completed.

1799

1801
Elector Max Franz dies, and Beethoven's letters to Wegeler mention increasing deafness.

16

Chapter Three

Reading Comprehension Questions

1. To whom does Herr Neefe encourage Ludwig to go for more musical instruction?
   • The great Mozart in Vienna, p. 72.
2. Why did it take Ludwig a long time to save enough money for a trip to Vienna?
   • He had to play special music at the palace to earn the extra money, p. 73; he dropped a coin while putting it in his savings box and lost it through a crack in the floor, p. 73; he used the money to help his family buy clothes and food, p. 76.
3. When Ludwig first played for Mozart in Vienna, was Mozart highly impressed by the lad? What finally captured Mozart's attention in Ludwig's playing, and what did he predict about Ludwig?
   • Mozart was not overly impressed at first. Vienna was filled with many other young men who played the keyboard as well as Ludwig, p. 78. When Ludwig began improvising a theme of Mozart's, however, Mozart's opinion changed, p. 79.
4. Why did Ludwig hurriedly return to Bonn from Vienna?
   • Mother Beethoven died and he had to earn a living for his father and brothers, p. 82.
5. Can you give the names of at least two dear friends from this chapter who helped Ludwig out in times of need or exhaustion?
   • Stephen Breuning, a pupil, p. 82; Count Waldstein, p. 86; Prince Lichnowsky in Vienna, p. 88; and Wegeler, a friend, p. 95.
6. Ludwig was again allowed to move to Vienna to continue his music studies. From what famous composer did Ludwig begin taking lessons when he returned to Vienna?
   • Joseph Haydn, p. 88.
7. Ludwig was soon called upon to give concerts for many of the prince's friends, but this was a struggle for Ludwig. Why did he feel he needed to leave the palace?
   • He was overwhelmed and couldn't find the time to compose as he wished, p. 95. He also did not like having to dress carefully, care for his beard, attend dinner at four, and so forth, p. 95.

8. By the end of this chapter, what physical struggle was Ludwig fighting, and how did he respond to it as it worsened?
• Sickness had settled in his ears so that they buzzed continually, and he couldn't hear clearly, p. 100. He determined to leave Vienna before his friends knew he was going deaf, p. 101.

Character Qualities

Frugality (pp. 73, 88, 96) – Ludwig carefully saved any extra pennies he earned from playing special music, with the hopes of using the money for a trip to Vienna to study under Mozart. He was very frustrated at losing even one coin from his savings box. He even rode in an open coach to Vienna to save money, p. 76. When he moved to Vienna permanently (somewhat permanently, at least), Ludwig was willing to live in an attic room offered by a generous prince so that his expenses were diminished a bit more.

Passionate Determination (pp. 77–79, 82, 95) – Ludwig's eyes burned with his passion for music, and he was determined to show Mozart that he was more than just a decent pianist. Mozart was impressed by Ludwig's spirit and musical power, p. 79. After returning

home from Vienna, Ludwig was determined to provide for his family's needs after his mother's death — to the point that he overworked himself and became ill from a lack of food and rest. Furthermore, Ludwig's *music* displayed his passion. He wrote with emotion and ignored "rules" in order to share the thoughts that burned in his mind. He was equally determined to cope with his deafness on his own, p. 101.

Creativity (pp. 79, 95) – Mozart recognized Ludwig's creative genius at their first meeting when Ludwig improvised richly on a Mozart melody. Mozart told his friends to keep an eye on Ludwig: "He will make a noise in the world some day." When Ludwig began studying under Albrechtsberger and Salieri, they scolded him for not following the rules of composition in his works, but Ludwig argued that he needed to write the music as he felt it, as it sang itself in his head.

Tidbits of Interest

Page 69 – Beethoven ate a bowl of porridge before leaving for the Easter services. Perhaps your children would enjoy a bowl of porridge while you read Chapter Three.

Slow-Cooker Porridge Recipe

¼ c. cracked wheat	½ c. raisins
¾ c. rolled oats (not instant oatmeal)	¼ c. wheat germ
3 c. water	½ c. apple, grated
¼ tsp. cinnamon	Milk and honey

Combine all ingredients up to milk and honey in slow-cooker. Turn to lowest setting. Cook overnight. Spoon into bowls, and serve with milk and honey.

Page 70 – The walls of defense around Bonn were first built in 1244. The "guns" mentioned here are cannons — fired in salute on Easter Day.

Pages 71–72 – Many considered Ludwig a piano virtuoso by age eleven.[21] But when Ludwig was about fifteen or sixteen, Master Neefe encouraged him to go on for more training under a new master. Beethoven later wrote Master Neefe a letter of gratitude, stating: "I thank you for the counsel which you gave me so often in my progress in my divine art. If I ever become a great man yours shall be a share of the credit."[22]

Pages 73–76 – No wonder Ludwig's travel fund didn't grow very rapidly; he was busy supplying as much as he could for his family's needs! It is probable that Ludwig's mother was already suffering from tuberculosis (sometimes called consumption) before Ludwig's trip to Vienna. In addition, she had an infant daughter named Margaret for whom to care.[23] She needed rest and proper food to recover from this bacterial disease of the lungs.

Page 76 – Ludwig finally received the passage money he needed from the Elector for his coach ride to Vienna in 1787. Vienna was the capital of Austria on the Danube River, and it was the seat of the Hapsburg empire (1806–1867). Vienna was also a city of music, even described as the musical center of the world.

Page 78 – Ludwig is described as having unkempt hair when he first approached Mozart. The style of the day was careful pigtails, but Ludwig let his thick hair grow long and wild — his entire life.[24] Mozart initially recognized Ludwig as a good pianist, but at that time Vienna had hundreds of good pianists. Amazingly enough, during Beethoven's time, Vienna had some 200,000 residents, of whom at least 6,000 were pianists![25]

Page 79 – Improvisation is composing on the spur of the moment, or making and arranging offhand. It was Ludwig's improvisation that led to Mozart's prophetic comment about Ludwig making a noise in the world some day. Beethoven later said that Mozart had "a fine but choppy way of playing" because the manner of playing required for a clavier or a harpsichord was different than that demanded for piano, and Beethoven's interest was in the piano.[26] It appears Ludwig was in Vienna for only two weeks before returning to Bonn because his father had written that his mother was dying.[27]

Page 82 – Maria Beethoven died July 17, 1787, shortly after Ludwig's return to Bonn. When she died, Ludwig wrote, "She was such a kind, loving mother to me, and my best friend."[28] Sadly, four months later Ludwig's seven-month-old sister (Margaret) also died. Ludwig was only seventeen, and a year that started with hope and joy was ending in despair, sorrow, and bitterness. He became exhausted, and a pupil, Stephen Breuning, took Ludwig home to his family. Ludwig had given music lessons to two of the von Breuning children. The von

Breunings were a wealthy and generous family, and they talked with Beethoven about art, science, politics, and literature. Stephen continued to help Ludwig at many low moments in his life.

Page 86 – It was probably at the von Breunings' home that Beethoven first met Count Ferdinand Ernst Gabriel Waldstein (1762–1823). Count Waldstein later introduced Beethoven's musical genius to the Austrian nobles of Vienna. He became Ludwig's most important supporter (aside from the Elector), and he helped introduce Ludwig to the famed composer Joseph Haydn (1732–1802) who passed through

Bonn in 1790 in his way to London, and again on his return from London in 1792.

Page 87 – Franz Joseph Haydn was Austria's premier composer of the time, supported by the Esterhazy family for most of his career. He was particularly known for his symphonies (108 of them), and he was a primary shaper of Classical style music. Ludwig wrote a new composition, a cantata, to commemorate the recent death of Emperor Joseph II in 1790, which he then gave to Haydn to critique. His work so impressed the older composer (sometimes called Papa Haydn) that he offered to teach the young musician.

Page 88 – In 1792, Ludwig made his second trip to Vienna, but travel to that city was not so safe now because of the growing conflict that started in France three years before (the French Revolution). Commoners in Paris had revolted against the rulers, and they deposed King Louis XVI in 1792. Austria (and other European countries) sided with the imprisoned king, declaring war against the French people. Two years after Ludwig left Bonn, in fact, the French invaded the city, causing Elector Maximilian Franz to flee the city and never return.[29] Nevertheless, Vienna was a better location for success musically than any other city in the Hapsburg empire because Vienna's imperial family and several other wealthy families supported musicians in Vienna. In the years that Ludwig lived in Vienna, composers were becoming more appreciated in their own right as gifted artists, not as servants who had to write under a patron's demands or restrictions. Ludwig did receive help from many friends, however, including Prince Karl Lichnowsky, a musical aristocrat who had once studied with Mozart.[30] The prince offered Beethoven numerous opportunities to perform, gave him rooms to live in, and understood Ludwig's eccentricities.

Page 90 – Ludwig quickly "made his reputation as the most exciting keyboard player in Vienna just at the time when the piano was beginning to replace the harpsichord."[31] Pianos were cheaper to make than harpsichords, and they allowed for greater dynamics, which suited Beethoven's style and music perfectly. Beethoven even introduced bent-finger playing to get more dynamics and character from the piano.

Pages 91–92 – The friend Cramer with whom Ludwig took walks was Jean Baptiste Cramer, a fellow composer, from London, who was using the piano's range and scope in a style independent of the Viennese school of music.[32] They heard the melodies of Mozart played throughout the city of Vienna. Mozart had died in 1791 and was buried in an unmarked pauper's grave.

Page 94 – Ludwig began studying with Haydn in late 1792 and continued through October of 1793. They shared cups of chocolate and coffee[33], and Haydn even loaned him money at one point.[34] However, Ludwig considered Haydn a poor teacher because Haydn was preoccupied with his own compositions for his second London journey.[35] Even so, Haydn wisely predicted, "…Beethoven will in time fill the position of one of Europe's greatest composers, and I shall be proud to be able to speak of myself as his teacher."[36]

Eventually, Beethoven decided to show his compositions to two new music masters: Johann Georg Albrechtsberger and Antonio Salieri. Albrechtsberger was a great musical theorist and disciplinarian who worked Beethoven hard, but Ludwig knew it was worth the effort to be able to express what was in his head, to get it on paper at last.[37] Salieri was a popular composer and the director of music (the Kapellmeister) at the imperial court in Vienna for thirty-six years. Ironically, Salieri "refused to recognize the value of Mozart and his works,"[38] and was known as Mozart's great rival. Yet, both Mozart and Salieri saw musical genius when they saw Beethoven before a keyboard.

Page 95 – Ludwig's burning emotions were played out in his music — even if that music went against the rules that Salieri and Albrechtsberger were teaching him. His compositions bridged the Classical achievements of the 18th century to the Romanticism of the 19th century. He moved music from its focus on form and rules (restraints from the Classical era) to the wildly emotional and personalized expression of the Romantic era. Franz Wegeler had been a young medical student in Bonn who had lived with the von Breuning family. He very likely introduced Ludwig to the von Breunings.[39]

Page 96 – Most contemporaries of Beethoven and biographers admit that Ludwig was very disorganized and even sloppy in his personal life and appearance. When his clothes became too dirty or tattered, his friends would snatch them in the night and replace them with new ones.[40] Once when he was at the height of his musical career in Vienna, he took a walk in such a disheveled state that he was arrested by a police officer who thought he was a tramp![41] Ludwig's first official public appearance as a composer occurred in March 1795 at the old Burg Theater in Vienna. He was twenty-four years old and immediately followed this debut with concert tours to Prague, Dresden, Leipzig, Berlin, and Hungary in 1796.

Page 98 – Wheeler mentions that practices with the orchestra began at 8 A.M. at the palace. Ludwig was an early riser who liked working in the morning, particularly composing in the early hours.

Page 99 – Ludwig often directed from his piano, but sometimes Ludwig became so involved in the music that he would forget he was a soloist, and jumping up from his piano, he would begin conducting in his own peculiar fashion.[42] His conducting style included leaping in the air in the loud parts, waving his arms to the skies, crouching in quiet parts (almost under the music stand), and later (during his deafness) even shouting out loud without being aware.[43] One time, another composer witnessed Ludwig conducting with such fury that "when he struck the first chord of the solo he broke six strings" on the piano.[44]

Page 100 – Vienna was very proud of its new composer, and many people wanted to take lessons from him, but he was an impatient and rather quarrelsome piano teacher. Moreover, weariness, exhaustion, and a raging fever caused by typhus in 1797 weakened his body.[45] By 1801, sickness settled in his ears, causing buzzing and ringing day and night. Ludwig later claimed that the shelling of Vienna by Napoleon Bonaparte's troops caused his deafness. His rooms were in line of the shelling, and he covered his head with pillows to shut out the noise.[46] Ludwig also claimed that exposure to cold caused his deafness, but it is more likely that his deafness was due to nerve damage from a combination of factors. The Doctor Schmidt who treated Ludwig was Johann Adam Schmidt, a professor of general pathology and therapy at Josephine Academy, and he was Beethoven's personal physician.[47]

Page 101 – Melancholy, loneliness, and pride or fear seem to have caused Ludwig to move from Vienna. He wrote his brothers that he felt his deafness meant he "must live as an exile."[48] Yet, in the midst of his struggles he sought God to make sense of life's unfairness: "Therefore, calmly will I submit myself to all inconsistency and will place all my confidence in your eternal goodness, O God! My soul shall rejoice in Thee, immutable Being. Be my rock, my light, forever my trust."[49]

1802 – 1827

Beethoven writes letter (known as the Heiligenstadt Testament) to his brothers to share his despair over his deafness. He completes his Second Symphony. — **1802**

1804 — Beethoven changes the dedication of his Third Symphony from one to Napoleon to *Eroica* when Napoleon crowns himself Emperor.

Beethoven works on his opera *Fidelio*. The French invade Vienna. — **1805**

1806 — Beethoven's nephew Karl is born to his younger brother Karl. Beethoven completes the Fourth Symphony.

Beethoven is offered the post of Kapellmeister in the King of Westphalia's palace. He declines the offer when friends guarantee an annual income if he remains in Vienna. Beethoven completes Fifth and Sixth Symphonies. — **1808**

1811 — Austria is bankrupt. Beethoven experiences some financial difficulties because of the devaluation of currency.

Fidelio is revised. Beethoven's financial position improves when the Congress of Vienna grants him 4000 florins. — **1814**

1815 — Brother Karl Beethoven dies and Beethoven becomes guardian of his nephew Karl. The Congress of Vienna closes.

Beethoven's friendship with Nanette Streicher is renewed. She helps Beethoven with domestic concerns. — **1817**

1819 — *Missa Solemnis*, a mass by Beethoven, is begun. Beethoven establishes an inheritance, or legacy, for Karl.

Beethoven begins work on the Choral (Ninth) Symphony, which he completes in 1824. — **1822**

1826 — Beethoven visits his brother's estate, but he catches a chill on his return to Vienna. Beethoven is confined to bed, and his final illness begins.

Beethoven dies on March 26. He is buried March 29 in Vienna. — **1827**

Chapter Four

Reading Comprehension Questions

1. What did Beethoven do in Heiligenstadt to help him forget about his deafness? There are numerous possible answers.

   • He wore his favorite old coat, went for walks in the meadows and mountains, ran through the rains, sat beneath trees to compose, and let the music in his mind carry him away, pp. 103, 105.

2. What did Beethoven keep around his neck to help him communicate with others around him?

   • A little pad of paper, or a notebook, on which to write, p. 104.

3. How did the world of nature seem to help Beethoven with his music?

   • Nature offered him peace, and helped him to remember sounds so that he could write out melodies in his notebook, pp. 107, 116.

4. Can you provide a story or anecdote from this chapter that shows Beethoven was not always careful with things or mindful of things, especially when he was composing? There are numerous proofs for this idea of absent-mindedness.

   • He stomped and pounded around the room, upsetting ink on the piano, p.106; he danced away from a festival, waving his arms to the music in his head, p. 110; he greeted dinner guests in a nightcap and apron, pp. 117–118; his rooms were in disarray, with boots wrapped in music, p. 118; his pianos had no legs because he moved so often, p. 119; he poured cold water on his head while he composed, but he didn't consider that it would leak through to apartments below his, p. 120–121.

5. When Beethoven returned to Vienna, what young boy greeted him near his front door?

   • His nephew Karl, who had been left in Beethoven's care when Karl's father died, p. 133.

6. What beverage did Beethoven enjoy, especially before sunrise?

   • Coffee — sixty beans per cup, p. 135.

7. How do we know that Vienna never forgot Beethoven even in the midst of his struggle with deafness?

   • They asked him to give the premier performances of his Ninth Symphony and Mass, *Missa Solemnis*, for them, p.140. Moreover, they applauded and waved their handkerchiefs to him to show their appreciation at the close of the concert, p. 143.

Character Qualities

Appreciated Nature (pp. 103–104, 107, 116) – Ludwig reveled in going for walks in the mountains and meadows where he could feel the wind and see the trees. Neither thunderstorms nor darkness deterred him from these walks. (He might have been an excellent postman if he had not continued with music, eh?) He found peace in the stars, clouds, and trees, and they all helped him to remember sounds for his melodies. At one point he felt that even the trees were crying out, "Holy! Holy!" (By the way, Isaiah 55:12 indicates that this is not a far-fetched notion at all.)

Generous (pp. 117, 134, 140, 144) – Beethoven welcomed friends to his home (though he was in a nightcap and offered watery soup for supper). He welcomed his needy nephew Karl into his home and provided for his needs, setting aside a large gift he had received specifically for Karl's education. Ludwig gave a first-performance concert of his Ninth Symphony and Mass to the people of Vienna, a rare appearance at this stage in his deafness. And he gave music for generation upon generation to enjoy and cherish.

Moody (pp. 118–119, 121, 136, 144) – Beethoven was a man of emotional extremes, and that emotion was expressed in his music. Whether it was frustration over the conditions of his home, irritation at the poor service he obtained from his hired help, or anger at being interrupted by his landlady, he was quick to express his opinion and feelings. He was sensitive to the emotions of others, too, such as his response to the blind girl when he composed his *Moonlight Sonata* and his humble reply to the praise of the people of Vienna at the final concert.

Tidbits of Interest

Page 103 – On the advice of Dr. Schmidt, Beethoven went to Heiligenstadt, a village north of Vienna that was famous for its sulfur springs and its views of the Danube River and Carpathian Mountains. You will want to decide for yourself whether or not to share that this visit to Heiligenstadt started as a low point in Beethoven's life. Wheeler politely avoids mentioning Beethoven's initial depression regarding his deafness. At one point he even contemplated suicide, but his desire to produce music ("Art") held him back from such a drastic choice.[50] He would not remain silent in his world of silence. In fact, it was in

Heiligenstadt that Beethoven wrote his dear friend Wegeler in 1801 insisting, "I will seize Fate by the throat; it shall certainly not bend and crush me completely."[51]

Pages 103, 107 – Ludwig loved walks in the out-of-doors, regardless of the weather. Max Ring, a doctor who once visited Ludwig at one of his summer residences, described him as "not quite right in his mind; he would often run, bareheaded, without a hat, around in the great park…hours on end, even if it were raining with lightning and thunder."[52]

Page 104 – Beethoven used small notebooks that could fit in his pocket or hang from his neck so that he could document musical ideas when he was away from home. He would stitch together these notebooks himself since ready-made musical manuscript notebooks were too expensive.[53] He would sometimes mull over the musical ideas or "sketches" noted in the booklets for years before developing them into composition building blocks. As his deafness increased, the small notebooks also became "conversation notebooks" in which visitors could write what they wanted to ask Beethoven or what they wanted him to know.

Page 105 – Beethoven claimed he was too clumsy to sharpen a quill, and his broad fingers weren't suited for sharpening and using a regular pencil because the point broke too quickly.[54] He chose to use a carpenter's pencil with its broad, thick lead.

Page 107 – Beethoven used a number of different ear trumpets, also called acoustic cornets, in an effort to hear more clearly. Some of those trumpets were designed and constructed by Johann Nepomuk Maelzel, a Czech who is also believed to have been the inventor of the metronome used to keep a regular tempo in music. Ludwig's Fifth Symphony is a musical depiction of his struggle with deafness.[55]

Pages 110–116 – Essentially, this section is describing Ludwig's inspiration and process of writing the five movements of the *Pastoral* (or Sixth) Symphony. It is the only symphony for which Beethoven gave a program, suggesting that it was scenes from life in the country. Some believe that the *Pastoral* Symphony was truly the start of Romantic music — full of emotion, surprise, and personal expression.[56]

Page 118 – Ludwig was notorious for his poor cooking skills. He liked macaroni and cheese (didn't know it had been around so long, did you?), red herrings, and a mushy soup of bread and eggs.[57] He was also a notoriously poor housekeeper. He moved nearly eighty times in his thirty-five years in Vienna!

Page 119 – His pianos were without legs because he moved so often. It has also been suggested that by placing the piano on the floor, lying on the floor, and holding a stick with his teeth to the frame of the piano Ludwig could feel the sound vibrations.[58] Pianos in Beethoven's day were made with wooden frames, rather than metal ones like today, which meant they were more fragile. The wooden frames also meant they could support less tension on the strings, so they made less sound than modern pianos. At least four of Beethoven's pianos were gifts from piano manufacturers.[59] One of those piano manufacturers may have given him contact with Nanette Streicher, the daughter of a piano factory owner and a musical prodigy in her own right. Frau Streicher and Beethoven had been friends for some time. In 1817, Ludwig wrote Streicher sixty letters asking for her help in coping with the mundane things in life — cooking, laundry, hiring servants, changing lodgings, and other domestic matters.[60]

Pages 119–120 – Ludwig nearly took the post of senior musician or Kapellmeister for the King of Westphalia, Jerome Bonaparte, Napoleon's brother, who ruled in Westphalia from 1807–1813. Three Viennese aristocrats combined their resources to offer Ludwig a salary for life if he remained in Vienna.[61] The Napoleonic Wars made this arrangement difficult to fulfill, but Beethoven was never penniless, though he never had much money after the Congress of Vienna in 1815.[62] Oh, and Ludwig *did* pour pitchers of water over his head to stay cool and stay awake — much to his landlords' annoyance.

Page 128 – *Fidelio* was Ludwig's only opera. Napoleon's troops marched into Vienna and shelled the city one week before the opera's opening.[63] Some people consider it among the greatest operas, but Ludwig rarely wrote well for voices because he treated them as just another musical instrument, so he often ignored the limitations of the human voice.[64] *Fidelio* was written in honor of the Congress of Vienna (1814–1815) in which Europe's leaders met with the aim of stamping out current revolutionary ideas, putting an end to Napoleon's political influence, and restoring old political orders. Beethoven's Third Symphony, incidentally, was originally to be dedicated to Napoleon, because Beethoven had idealized him as a hero of humanity, leading mankind into an age of liberty, equality, and fraternity (the ideals of the French Revolution). When Beethoven learned that Napoleon had crowned himself emperor, Beethoven ripped up the dedication page and renamed it *Eroica* (*Heroic*) in honor of the heroic "common man."

Page 129 – Beethoven invited Stephen von Breuning to Baden, a place of cures and relaxation. Stephen nursed Beethoven through illnesses, came alongside him during his anger and humiliation in his deafness, and had even helped the composer pull *Fidelio* into shape from its original 1805 production.[65] While the spas in Baden did not lessen his deafness, Beethoven began composing harder than ever. His musical excellence and creativity seemed to burst forth even more in his world of increasing silence (1802–1816). It is believed he was completely deaf by 1817, but in those fourteen years of deepening deafness, Beethoven wrote six symphonies, an overture, an opera, two piano concertos, piano sonatas, and quartets.

Page 131 – It is intriguing to note how Wheeler uses bells chiming in each chapter to tie the story of Beethoven's life together — from the carillon in Bonn to the tower bells in Vienna. Trace this strand of chiming bells in pages 19, 35, 69, 131, and 141, and talk with your children about how well-crafted stories will have threads and ideas carefully woven throughout a story. This concept also gives the book's title even more meaning.

Page 133 – Ludwig's younger brother Karl developed tuberculosis (just as his mother had) and left guardianship or care of his son with Beethoven. Nephew Karl was nine years old and Ludwig was forty-seven when they began dwelling in the same house. While their relationship was often rather stormy, Beethoven never failed to do whatever he needed to do to provide for his nephew's needs.[66]

Page 135 – Ludwig loved strong coffee. (Sixty beans per cup seems like a caffeine-fix for a full day!) He also enjoyed afternoons at a coffeehouse where he could read the newspaper and share in local gossip.[67] Gerhardt von Breuning (1813–1892) was Stephen's son. Beethoven called Gerhardt "Trouser-button" and was interested in his musical education.

Page 137 – *Moonlight Sonata* is perhaps the most recognized piano sonata in history. The piano was central to Beethoven's art. He composed thirty-two piano sonatas.

Page 140 – Beethoven's Ninth Symphony, called *Choral*, is set to a poem entitled "Ode to Joy" by Johann Christoph Friedrich von Schiller. Schiller was a German poet and playwright whose works championed the cause of political freedom.[68] The poem speaks of the brotherhood of man and the arrival of joy through suffering.[69] It is little wonder, then, that the Ninth Symphony was played during the Chinese student protest in Communist China in 1989 and during the fall of Germany's Berlin Wall, also in 1989.

Page 143 – At the close of Beethoven's final concert in Vienna, he cried when someone turned him to see the audience applauding — applause he could no longer hear.[70]

On March 26, 1827, Beethoven died of complications from pneumonia and liver failure. His final words were appropriately, "I shall hear in heaven."[71] Twenty thousand Viennese came to watch Beethoven's funeral procession[72] — that's one out of ten people in Vienna at the time.[73]

Patrick Kavanaugh's statement perhaps best summarizes Beethoven's life: "The judgment of a man's greatness is not only to be measured in the mission he accomplishes but in the obstacles he has overcome in the process."[74] Beethoven overcame innumerable difficulties to give mankind music of passion, joy, and emotion that has been cherished by every subsequent musical age.

Endnotes

[1] H.C. Robbins Landon, *Beethoven: A Documentary Study* (New York: Macmillan Publishing Co., Inc., 1974), 23.

[2] Ibid., 25.

[3] Patrick Kavanaugh, *Spiritual Lives of the Great Composers* (Grand Rapids, MI: Zondervan, 1996), 60.

[4] Ibid., 58.

[5] Landon, *Beethoven: A Documentary Study*, 25.

[6] Ibid., 29.

[7] Ibid.

[8] Ibid., 23.

[9] Ibid., 26.

[10] Maynard Solomon, *Beethoven* (New York: Schirmer Books, 1977), 17.

[11] Kathleen Krull, *Lives of the Musicians: Good Times, Bad Times* (San Diego, CA: Harcourt, Inc., 1993), 25.

[12] Jane Stuart Smith and Betty Carlson, *The Gift of Music: Great Composers and Their Influence* (Wheaton, IL: Crossway Books, 1995), 61.

[13] Ibid., 63.

[14] Pam Brown, *The World's Greatest Composers: Ludwig van Beethoven,* United Kingdom: Exley Publications Ltd., 1993), 24.

[15] Solomon, *Beethoven*, 18.

[16] Brown, *The World's Greatest Composers: Ludwig van Beethoven,* 11.

[17] Kavanaugh, *Spiritual Lives of the Great Composers*, 58.

[18] Krull, *Lives of the Musicians: Good Times, Bad Times,* 25.

[19] Brown, *The World's Greatest Composers: Ludwig van Beethoven,* 12.

[20] O.G. Sonneck, *Beethoven: Impressions by His Contemporaries* (New York: Dover Publications, Inc., 1967), 10.

[21] Samuel Nisenson and William DeWitt, *Illustrated Minute Biographies* (New York: Grosset & Dunlap, 1953), 22.

[22] Brown, *The World's Greatest Composers: Ludwig van Beethoven,* 12.

[23] Ibid., 18.

[24] Krull, *Lives of the Musicians: Good Times, Bad Times,* 27.

[25] Barbara Nichol, *Beethoven Lives Upstairs* (Ontario, Canada: Classical Kids Recordings, 1989), CD insert notes.

[26] Brown, *The World's Greatest Composers: Ludwig van Beethoven,* 15.

[27] Ibid., 17.

[28] Ibid.

[29] Roland Vernon, *Introducing Beethoven* (Parsippany, NJ: Silver Burdett Press, 1996), 12.

[30] Ibid., 15.

[31] Ibid.

[32] Landon, *Beethoven: A Documentary Study*, 56.

[33] Ates Orga, *Beethoven: His Life and Times* (Neptune City, NJ: Paganiniana Publications, Inc., 1980), 45.

[34] Landon, *Beethoven: A Documentary Study,* 37, 39.

[35] Ibid., 37.

[36] Ibid., 39.

[37] Brown, *The World's Greatest Composers: Ludwig van Beethoven*, 24.

[38] Landon, *Beethoven: A Documentary Study,* 43.

[39] Brown, *The World's Greatest Composers: Ludwig van Beethoven*, 14.

[40] Krull, *Lives of the Musicians: Good Times, Bad Times,* 27.

[41] Kavanaugh, *Spiritual Lives of the Great Composers*, 56.

[42] Brown, *The World's Greatest Composers: Ludwig van Beethoven*, 53.

[43] Krull, *Lives of the Musicians: Good Times, Bad Times,* 28.

[44] Brown, *The World's Greatest Composers: Ludwig van Beethoven,* 53.

[45] Ibid., 26.

[46] Nichol, *Beethoven Lives Upstairs*, CD insert notes.

[47] Solomon, *Beethoven*, 114.

[48] Kavanaugh, *Spiritual Lives of the Great Composers*, 57.

[49] Maynard Solomon, *Beethoven Essays* (Cambridge: Harvard University Press, 1988), 218.

[50] Smith and Carlson, *The Gift of Music*, 63.

[51] Brown, *The World's Greatest Composers: Ludwig van Beethoven,* 36.

[52] Landon, *Beethoven: A Documentary Study*, 115.

[53] James Wierzbicki, "The Beethoven Sketchbooks," *St. Louis Post-Dispatch*, Jan. 5, 1986.

[54] Dr. Gerhard von Breuning, *From the Schwarzspanier House: My Boyhood Memories of Beethoven* (Vienna: L. Rosner, 1874), 37.

[55] Smith and Carlson, *The Gift of Music*, 65.

[56] Ibid.

[57] Krull, *Lives of the Musicians: Good Times, Bad Times,* 27.

[58] Nichol, *Beethoven Lives Upstairs*, CD insert notes.

[59] Ibid.

[60] Solomon, *Beethoven*, 240.

[61] Vernon, *Introducing Beethoven*, 23.

[62] Landon, *Beethoven: A Documentary Study*, 131.

[63] Nichol, *Beethoven Lives Upstairs*, CD insert notes.

[64] Smith and Carlson, *The Gift of Music*, 64.

[65] Brown, *The World's Greatest Composers: Ludwig van Beethoven,* 42.

[66] Ibid., 57.

[67] Krull, *Lives of the Musicians: Good Times, Bad Times,* 28.

[68] Vernon, *Introducing Beethoven*, 31.

[69] Smith and Carlson, *The Gift of Music*, 65.

[70] Krull, *Lives of the Musicians: Good Times, Bad Times,* 28.

[71] Brown, *The World's Greatest Composers: Ludwig van Beethoven,* 60.

[72] Vernon, *Introducing Beethoven*, 29.

[73] Krull, *Lives of the Musicians: Good Times, Bad Times,* 29.

[74] Kavanaugh, *Spiritual Lives of the Great Composers*, 61.